The Camera Doesn't Lie!

Written by Mary-Anne Creasy

Flying Start
to Literacy®

Contents

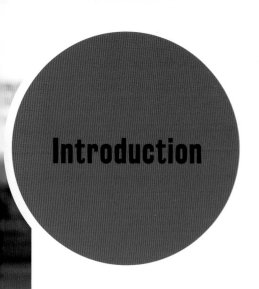

Introduction

This is Mike Curtain. He is a professional photographer. Mike has taken photos of food, cars, animals, babies, celebrities, sports stars and more. He has also taken photos for children's books like this one to make the book more appealing and to help the reader understand the story.

Mike has been a professional photographer for more than 20 years and has seen many changes in photography. Computer technology has made anything possible in a photo. The expression "The camera doesn't lie" used to be true – what you saw in a photo was real. But these days, is it still possible to claim that?

Chapter 1

Photography and technology

Everyone can take photos because we've got cameras in our phones. We can take a photo and put it on social media instantly to show our friends what we are doing, or we can email or text it to someone, or just store it on a computer. The photos most people take are just for fun and they usually don't think about the lighting, the angle, how things are positioned or even if there are too many things in the photo.

The photos I take are different. I take time to position things or people before I take the photo, and I'll only include what's necessary for the image to look good. I know how to put the right amount of light into a photo; I use the appropriate lens and the best angle. All these things are important when I'm trying to make my client's product or business look better than everyone else's.

Computer technology makes everything possible. After a photo shoot, I use computer software to upload the photos, and to adjust the colours and lighting slightly. The client will then choose which images they want to use. I'll put these images into a special computer program, which can do almost anything. It can turn a blue car red, or make a cloudy day look sunny. I can even put different eyes on someone's face, which is especially useful if I've taken a group photo and one person has their eyes closed!

I can also take things out of a photo or move things around. In fact, there's not much you can't change in a photo.

Sometimes it's frustrating because people know about the abilities of computer software in photography, so they expect everything to look perfect in the photo, especially how they look. I want clients to look great in photos, so I'll often smooth off a few lines and wrinkles. But I've had clients complain about how they look, wanting me to make significant changes to their appearance. One client wanted me to give her a fringe!

Sometimes I spend more time on the computer, manipulating and adjusting images, than I do actually taking photos.

Chapter 2

Getting good shots

What is the most difficult thing you have had to photograph?

Sometimes the most difficult things to photograph are people. Most people hate having their photo taken. I try to make them feel relaxed or they won't look good in the photo. Small children are hard to photograph because they don't understand what's happening and they don't like to sit still. Animals are probably the most difficult, because you really can't control them.

Once, I did a difficult shoot for a children's book showing a dog eating a doughnut. Doughnuts are not a healthy food so, of course, we only wanted to feed the dog the one doughnut. But the dog loved the doughnut and ate it so quickly that there was no time to take the photo. We tried a few times to take the photo, but each time he gobbled the doughnut down in one bite. He ended up having several doughnuts! Eventually he was not as hungry and ate more slowly. And I got the great shot I wanted!

How do you get a photo looking down on something?

For really high shots I'll go up in a helicopter, and strap myself into a special harness. Wearing a harness allows me to lean out of the helicopter to take photos. This is not unusual when working for a client who wants photos of land for a future housing development.

But once I had to do something a bit more dangerous. A client wanted photos to show their buildings and the land looking directly down from a long way up. I had to go up in a powerful helicopter to about 900 metres, the same height as the aeroplanes that were coming in to land at the airport. We were on their flight paths so we had to be fast.

I was wearing a harness with an extension lead so I could lean way out of the helicopter. This allowed me to get perfect shots of the land and buildings directly below. It was freezing cold at that altitude, and windy.

As soon as I was done, we had to descend quickly to get out of the flight paths. It felt like we were on a roller coaster!

For lower shots, I'll hire a cherry picker. Sometimes a client wants to sell apartments that will have great views before they have been built. So I take photos from a cherry picker of the area where the apartments will be built. These photos show the likely views from the apartments, and the images are used in advertising to attract buyers.

Photographers are also using drones now and I'm thinking about buying one for my business. Having a drone would mean I wouldn't have to hire a cherry picker or go up in a helicopter as often, which can be both risky and expensive.

Drones can get into smaller spaces where a helicopter or cherry picker wouldn't be practical. I could also attach a video camera to the drone, which would be ideal for videoing a sporting event like a surfing competition because it wouldn't be as intrusive as a big, noisy helicopter.

Chapter 3

Tricky photography

What's it like doing food photography?

Food photography can be tricky. Real food is sometimes not easy to control and does not look good in a photo. I work with people called food stylists who know lots of secrets about how to get food looking perfect for a photo.

I had a client who wanted me to take photos of a barbecued steak. A cooked steak shrinks and looks shrivelled. We cooked a steak very quickly so the barbecue grill marks appeared.

Then the food stylist painted the steak with soy sauce so it appeared cooked. In the photo you would never guess that the steak was almost raw inside!

There are many more food styling secrets used in photography. The ice blocks you see in a photo of a drink are cubes of clear plastic, which are especially made for food photography. And the sheen on the glass to make the drink look cold is spray-on deodorant.

The milk you see in cereal isn't milk because that would make the cereal look soggy, so food stylists will use sunscreen or even white glue.

Once I had a client who made ice cream toppings, and they wanted to show their product being poured onto ice cream. Ice cream melts quickly, so the food stylist made fake ice cream out of canned frosting and icing sugar. It looks like the real thing, but I could take as long as I wanted to set up the shot without worrying about the "ice cream" melting.

Taking photos of food can sometimes be frustrating, especially if I'm feeling hungry. I have to remind myself – don't take a bite!

How important is the weather?

The weather is important for outdoor photo shoots. Sometimes I'll contact the weather bureau to find out exactly what the prediction "fine but partly cloudy" means on the weather report. I need to know how much cloud they predict.

If I've organised lots of people and equipment for the shoot, paid for a location and then the weather lets me down, it's a disaster. I've sometimes had to cancel shoots the day before because we couldn't take the risk of even a slight chance of rain.

Before

After

There are always times when unexpected weather happens. Once, at the end of a long day's shoot, when I needed one last photo of a boy and a dog, it began to rain. We didn't stop because I didn't want to arrange the shoot again, as well as pay everyone involved, for only one photo. I put a torch behind the boy and dog, out of the shot, to make it look like the sun was shining. Then afterwards, on the computer, I removed the raindrops and added some yellow to the photo to make it look warm and sunny.

Chapter 4

Memorable shoots

What's been the best photography experience of your career?

I went to Burma / Myanmar for a client who needed some images to promote a company they planned to establish there. Not many people visit this country and it's hard to travel around once you arrive. We saw some amazing scenery and I got to take some great photos of things I've never seen before.

The best day was when I got up before sunrise to take photos in a hot-air balloon as the sun was coming up. The balloon was hovering above hundreds of temples scattered across an incredible landscape. It was so beautiful that I'll always remember it.

What is your most memorable shoot?

One shoot I'll never forget was taking photographs of reptiles at a wildlife park for a children's book. I was nervous taking photos of crocodiles from inside their enclosure, even though an expert crocodile handler was nearby. I knew that if you're not paying attention, or look away for an instant, a crocodile can spring forward and grab you. I had to get close and concentrate and try to forget that I was near a deadly predator. When you're looking through a lens, you can't see what's happening around you and I had to trust the handler who was responsible for my safety.

Next, I took photos of an enormous python. In the wild these snakes kill their prey by squeezing it to death and then eating it whole. I took photos of the handler holding the snake, and then I asked to hold the snake. It was really long and heavy and began to slide up around my neck. Then before I realised what was happening, I felt the snake begin to squeeze. The handler was able to get it off me, but it did scare me.

Chapter 5

Photography: Then and now

How has photography changed since you began your career?

When I started we used film, which was expensive, because there was a maximum of 36 images on each roll of film. We always had to have plenty of film with us on a shoot. The film was sent to a lab to be developed into photos, so you couldn't see the photos for a few hours, or even until the next day. Today, we use digital cameras and can take as many photos as we like. The only thing to worry about is running out of memory in the camera.

When I began, lighting, hair, make-up – in fact everything – had to be perfect the moment that a photo was taken, because it could not be changed later on a computer. On a shoot today, I link the camera to a laptop or a tablet and clients can see the photos as I take them. They can tell me if they are happy, or if any changes need to be made.

Mike's tips

How to take better photos

Cheaper digital cameras have made photography more accessible and today everyone can be a photographer! There are also lots of photography software apps and programs that people can use to digitally manipulate their own photos to make them look better.

It usually takes years of experience to become a good photographer. Having good artistic talent and an understanding of light is something that doesn't happen automatically when you pick up a camera.

Here are some of my tips!

- Don't be lazy! Crouch down to the eyeline of your subject before you take the photo.

- Don't use a camera phone to do close-ups of faces. The wide-angle lens distorts faces and makes noses look big.

- When photographing someone outside, try to avoid harsh direct light as that will make shadows and your subject will probably squint.

- Don't take photos looking into the sun. Try to have the sun behind you.

- Keep the background simple and uncluttered.

- A good tip for taking photos with a camera phone at night is to turn off your flash and get someone to shine a phone torch onto the subject, then take the photo.

I love being a photographer. I take photos of such a huge range of things, so it's never boring. I get to meet interesting people, and I have been able to travel to some amazing places.